HOW TO STOP DRINKING ALCOHOL

The Five Best Ways to Quit Drinking

ROBERT SMITH

© Copyright 2021 - All rights reserved.

It is not legal to reproduce, duplicate, or transmit any part of this document in either electronic means or in printed format. Recording of this publication is strictly prohibited and any storage of this document is not allowed unless with written permission from the publisher except for the use of brief quotations in a book review.

Contents

Introduction	v
1. Why Do We Drink?	1
2. Do You Have an Alcohol Problem?	9
3. The Effects of Alcohol on Health	17
4. Making the Decision not to Drink	25
5. What Do You Have to Change?	31
6. The First Method—Eliminating the Trigger	37
7. Finding Replacements	45
8. The 24-Hour Plan	51
9. When the Going Gets Tough	57
10. The Most Difficult Step	65
11. The Life of Your Dreams	73
Afterword	79
Bibliography	83

Introduction

Let's start from the beginning. What is it like to be an alcoholic? Jean, a recovering alcoholic, shares her journey in the following way:

"Hello, I'm Jean, one of the few fortunate alcoholics who have lived to share their story. I started drinking at an early age and was really popular in my high school days as a party animal. What started out as fun, ended as a nightmare. My drinking habits continued from high school to my workdays. My drinking was fairly under control. I thought I had the stamina to drink every night and work the next day. Slowly, I started to enter the vicious cycle. My life wasn't that bad. I had a beautiful home, a husband, and most of all, my lovely children. But as days passed, things started to get out of control. It was time for the fairytale to end. My husband left me and took my kids. I was thrown out of my house and got divorced. This was not the end of the misery. Eventually, I could no longer work. My pocket was empty and I had no money to pay for rent. My family also taught me the hard way. So, they did not allow me into their homes either. I was shattered and broken. I blamed everyone and everything. I don't even want my

enemies to feel what I felt. All this, just for some booze… The cost I paid was too much." (Verywellmind)[1]

This is a real-life story. Can you relate to this? If you are holding this book, then you can probably find yourself in this story somewhere. You can be at any stage of alcohol addiction, but the consequences are never going to be very different. A thing about addiction is that you always think that you are in control. And when you understand that you are not, it is almost the end of the line. Let us take a broader look at alcohol addiction and get into some crazy statistics:

- According to the 2019 NSDUH, 14.5 million people ages 12 and above had alcohol use disorders (AUD).
- 95,000 people die every year from alcohol-related illnesses annually.
- More than 10% of U.S. children ages 17 and below live with a parent with AUD.
- In 2019, 43.1 percent of liver disease deaths involved alcohol. (National Institute of Alcohol Abuse and Alcoholism, n.d.)[2]

When I tell people these stats, they are like, "C'mon Robert, I know people who have been drinking for years and are doing pretty well." Yes, but what are the odds? What are you risking your entire life for? What makes you think that you will not end up like Jean? Unfortunately, there are no statistics for calculating who is going to hit rock bottom and who is just going to retain their image of being a party animal. It is a gamble that you should not be willing to take. Knowingly and unknowingly, people fall back into the vicious cycle of this addiction. But how do you break the cycle?

This book is going to be your ultimate guide to breaking the vicious cycle of alcohol addiction. If you are reading the book, you probably have tried many other YouTube videos, attended motivational sessions, and made personal resolutions. Unfortunately, they have not worked out for you. The reason behind that is because changing a habit is not only about changing the routine of your actions, it also involves changing your mindset, your identity, and the way you look at life. In this book, I am going to touch on every aspect that will help you to create the ultimate mindset to break the addiction. All the theories and ways shared are not only based on research but I, myself have benefitted from these actions that I took to turn my life around. Without the five ways shared in this book, I would probably be in a bar drinking till I blacked out.

So how did I end up from being a drunk to changing my life around and being sober? Here is my story. I started drinking when I was 14. We all know how it starts. It's the night of a party when all of your friends want you to turn from a boy to a man. I was never an alcohol addict until my third year in college. My academic performance was poor, my mother and father got divorced, and my love life was a mess. The only time I felt better about myself was when I was drinking with my buddies. This turned to a habit loop that I continued for years. Now, when I look back to those years, I feel nothing but regret. I tried to make myself feel better but I was actually just too scared to face the failures in my life. My life was on autopilot. I got married and had a son. After the birth of my son, I tried to make resolutions that I would never drink anymore. But nothing really worked out for me, until my daughter was born.

My wife was in labor and I was too hung up to drive. I couldn't even think clearly when it happened. I was useless, and my 6-year-old son called our neighbors. They had to drive us to the hospital. Although I never considered myself as a great husband or a father, this broke me. I realized that I had reached the limit and it was time for a change. After thousands of hours of reading, research, and with multiple trial and errors, I found five ways that have changed my life forever. I now feel better as a husband, a father, and a human being. These methods have changed the way I think, how I feel, and how I live. I have not been drinking for the last seven years after using these methods.

But I was not the only one who benefited from them. These five methods have helped all my drinking buddies to turn their lives around and leave this vicious cycle within three months. They were all very skeptical about it, but I pushed them to give it a try. When my friends started to email me with their results, I was amazed. I thought it only worked for me, but no, these methods are universal and would work for anyone, anywhere. I have been preaching these methods ever since to every person who comes to me for counseling. Over thousands of people have benefitted from them. I can promise you that if you can implement and internalize the ways taught in this book, you will be able to stop drinking within three to six months. The cost of alcoholic addiction is too much, and I don't want anyone to pay the same price I paid. When I look back to my drinking days, I feel so much regret about the time I wasted. However, I feel grateful that I ended the cycle and I can now help others.

We should be in control of our lives and not the other way around. You have already wasted so many months, or maybe years trying to find a better version of yourself. This book is your chance to turn your wish into a reality. No more motivational speeches and New Years' resolutions. The time is now or never. Give yourself a nudge and dig into the five best ways to quit drinking.

ONE

Why Do We Drink?

WHEN YOU GO to a grocery store, how do you pick your food? Do you pick your food based on its nutrition or health values? No, you don't. In most cases, you pick it based on what it tastes like. But do people drink alcohol because it is tasty? Of course not. There are tons of reasons for drinking and taste is not one of them. Based on your age, gender, and your personal experience, you can have different reasons for drinking.

Escaping problems

This was why I was drinking and I know I was not alone. I have counseled many people over the years, and there were hundreds of them who had the same problem. They did not want to face their failures. Our lives are dynamic. They can be like roller coaster rides that have ups and downs throughout. But the fact that determines our success is not how we behave when we are living our highs, but rather how we face the lows. Everyone has friends and family who are there to lift them during their lows, but some still turn to alcohol. It feels like an emergency exit, a shortcut to taking your worries away. But in reality, it is just a broken exit. Mark Manson, in his book, *The Subtle Art of Not Giving a F**k*, describes this really well. He advises to look at happiness from a different angle. Happiness is not the absence of problems. No matter who we are and what we do, we all will have different problems. It is solving these problems that brings joy in our lives. You can never really delete all problems from your life, but you can replace your present problems with better outcomes.

Those of us who are trying to escape from failure and decline in our lives by drinking alcohol are only replacing our current problems with bigger and worse problems. The cycle of addiction is far more harmful than any other lows in your life. Drinking alcohol gives a momentary delusion of being happy and cheerful, a delusion which then quickly vanishes. When a person snaps out of this delusion, it could be too late.

Stress Relief

In the modern era, everyone faces stress and anxiety. The reason behind this is the huge expectations that we build into our lives. We feel we have to be better than everyone around us. We become competitive in every aspect of our lives. Trying to stay on top of the latest gadgets, the latest trends, the best car in the neighborhood, and the next promotion—all these wear us out. Alcohol can become one of our main stress relievers. It can slow down our central nervous system and give us a sense of relaxation. It alleviates the negative feelings and temporarily makes us feel happier and better about ourselves.

Although occasional alcohol consumption to relieve stress is not necessarily dangerous, it may influence us to drink more. Our neural receptors start to become resistant and need higher doses to relieve anxiety. This is usually how the habit loop begins in people who start drinking to relieve their stress. However, what people do not know is that prolonged periods of heavy drinking actually increase anxiety and stress.

Peer Pressure

We all want to blend into society. The idea of being accepted by everyone makes us feel better. This behavior is particularly common in teenagers, but adults are not much different. Drinking is a social norm that helps to form connections. Most teenagers have their first drink in front of their friends at a party.

I was no different. I started at a young age at my friend's birthday party. The atmosphere at those parties compels you to give alcohol a try. You don't want to be a boring lad in front of everyone. When you see all your friends are doing it, you want to belong to their crowd. Peer pressure is hard to resist, especially in a gathering when you don't want to feel left out. And yes, although most teenagers do not get addicted by drinking occasionally at parties, there are exceptions.

According to the Mayo Clinic, people who start drinking from an early age are more likely to get physical dependence as they get older (The Mayo Clinic 2018).[3] This is no surprise because we have already discussed how we need higher doses of alcohol to provide the same effect the longer we drink. Another reason we mostly fail to avoid peer pressure is our inability to say "no." We always think people are judging us by our behavior. Although that could be true, your true friends are not going to leave you just because you don't drink. Realizing this truth too late, you may succumb to addiction and become a heavy drinker.

Genetics

We have heard the phrase, "charity begins at home" but you should also know that "alcoholism can begin at home too". This is not to say that alcoholism is genetic, however. Drinking alcohol is always a choice which is influenced by a lot of factors, as we discussed previously. But genetics also plays an unavoidable role in alcoholism. If you look at most alcoholics' histories, one of the most important factors of risk development is their family history. One or both of their parents were alcoholics or heavy drinkers. Alcohol use disorders are linked to some specific genes. Having a close relative who is an alcoholic increases the chances of developing the addiction. In a study conducted by the National institute of Alcohol Abuse and Alcoholism, genetic factors were found to be between 40 and 60% responsible for the development of alcohol use disorder (National Institute of Alcohol Abuse and Alcoholism, n.d.).[2]

I know what you are thinking right now. If this disorder is genetic, there is nothing you can do to prevent it. That would be a completely wrong statement. As I have said earlier, drinking is always a choice and genetics is just one of the developmental factors. The reason I mentioned genetics to be one of the factors is because I want you to know that I have seen hundreds of people whose parents were both heavy drinkers, but they did not drink alcohol. They have learned from their parents' mistakes and changed their lives for the better. I have also seen the opposite, namely people whose parents were 100% sober, yet they drank heavily. They made their own choice.

If you are a heavy drinker, you probably drink or started drinking because of one of the above reasons. There could also be many other reasons for drinking, like traumatic experiences, lack of family support, and mental health disorders, among others. But no matter how you started, if you implement the methods discussed in this book, you are going to learn to suppress all your urges to drink. It doesn't matter where you start, but rather where you end up. Remember, no obstacle is too high and no path is too difficult to cross. If we want to avoid drinking once and for all, we need to have a clear idea about what really goes on in our heads when we drink. We all ask ourselves why we drink or why we cannot stop drinking. It is time to get some answers to these questions.

The Biology of Addiction

Addicted people lose control over their behavior. They seek and crave alcohol no matter what the cost. The true power of addiction lies in its power to hijack and destroy key brain regions that are supposed to help us survive. Alcohol activates the GABA neuron—the neuron responsible for inhibition of neural activity—and also inhibits glutamate, which is the counterpart responsible for the stimulatory actions of the brain. By inhibiting GABA neurons, it causes decreased central nervous system activity, which helps to relieve stress and anxiety in the short run (Harvard science review, n.d.).[3]

However, its long-term effects lie in the interference with the reward pathway in the brain. The reward pathway is what allows us to be happy and cheerful when we do something good for us. The key neurotransmitter responsible for this pathway is dopamine, which is released from a group of neurons in the midbrain. The proper functioning of the dopamine cycle helps us repeat behaviors or actions that make us happy, like spending time with loved ones, eating our favorite food, watching our favorite series, and so on. So how does alcohol influence the reward pathway? Alcohol increases the concentration of dopamine that stimulates desire in the body's reward center. So, when the body's reward center is stimulated, we tend to repeat the action as it makes us feel good even if it is by force. Simultaneously, alcohol binds to other neurotransmitters, like acetylcholine and serotonin, and alters their pathway.[4] Alterations in different pathways of the brain affect other regions of the brain. We are going to discuss more about this in Chapter 3.

We are not meant to always be happy. Our lives have ups and downs. The downs in our lives help us to appreciate the good in life. Alcohol is a drug that tries to hack the reward pathway and keep us in a bubble of euphoria and relief. Anxiety, stress, and sadness all are natural phenomena that every human deals with. Bypassing natural phenomena always has consequences. Consciousness altering drugs and alcohol act the same way. Bending our brain chemistry is not something we should engage in.

Chapter Summary

Here is what we learned from this chapter:

- The more you try to escape from a problem, the more you create a problem.
- Expectations can cause stress and anxiety.
- Peer pressure is real, but you can always say no.
- With sheer will and the right methods, you can defy genetics.
- Bending the physiological pathways for momentary pleasure can lead to disastrous consequences.

In the next chapter, you will learn to find out if you are addicted to alcohol or not.

TWO

Do You Have an Alcohol Problem?

ABOUT TWO THIRDS (66.3%) of adults over age 18 drink to some extent (Center for Disease Control and Prevention).[1] As you are reading this book, I would guess that you are one of them. But how can you guess if you are in control or are going in the right direction? All drinkers, even addicts, think they are in control of their drinking, but they are not. The problem with any kind of addiction is that it can escalate very fast. One month you are in control and suddenly within three months you can't spare a night without drinking. As a former alcoholic myself, I know how fast addiction gets you when you are not in control of your mind. How do you know if you are on the wrong path? Here are some red flags for you to identify.

How much is too much?

When I counsel people about stopping alcohol consumption, this is the question that I get asked the most often. There is no definitive answer here. In the U.S., a standard drink contains 14g of pure alcohol, which is typically found in 355 ml of regular beer, 150 ml of wine, or 45 ml of spirit (Alcohol Research Current Reviews, n.d.).[2] Keep in mind that different drinks have different alcohol contents. According to dietary guidelines for Americans, moderate drinking involves one drink per day for women and two drinks per day for men (U.S Department of Health and Human Services, n.d.).[3] Although the statistics show that one drink per day is safe, remember that those who drink regularly are far more likely to binge drink on daily basis.

Over the years, people have come to me and said, "Robert, I drink a lot but I don't feel too bad, I still feel in control." If you also feel this way, you should probably mark it as a red flag. All binge drinkers start with one drink. Next day they don't feel the same effect after one drink, so they drink two drinks. The wheel starts moving, and by the end of the year, they've doubled that. In conclusion, whenever you feel that you need more, you're having too much.

Denial

If you started reading this book yourself, then I would guess that you do not deny the fact that you are concerned about your drinking. However, alcoholics often deny that they could be in trouble. They are not willing to admit the reality of addiction. Although they might have already felt the bad physical effects of alcohol to some extent, they still deny it. You cannot prove to them they have a problem. Everyone around them can see that they are completely addicted to alcohol, and yet, they will try to defend their position saying, "I'm absolutely alright."

I remember every time I felt stomach pain, I never admitted that it was my drinking too much that caused it. I would blame something else, the food, the water, even the person preparing the food. Denial is the first step of self-defense. Overlooking the bad physical and mental effects that are clearly visible to others is a symptom that you are headed towards addiction.

Do you rationalize your drinking?

Rationalization by definition means to justify one's behavior. We all try to justify our acts, no matter if they are good or bad. Rationalizing is one of the defense mechanisms that provides an excuse to an action we know is wrong. It is easier to come up with excuses than to take the blame and accept responsibility. We blame our surroundings, our situation, and also the people in our lives for our behavior. Remember, rationalization of your drinking behavior is a big red flag that you are heading towards addiction.

We all know how drinking affects our body and mind. So we don't want to take responsibility for our ill actions. We may rationalize things by saying things like, " I don't drink because I want to, I drink because my marriage is a mess." Once a person becomes an alcoholic, all the reasons they provide are just excuses. I was guilty of doing this myself. When I started to drink heavily during my college years, I told myself that my life sucked and that's why I needed a drink. The gods did not bless me with enough good fortune, so drinking was what I did to make myself happy. But now I realize that whatever I did was just defending my own actions. If you are anything like me, stop putting the blame on the universe and take charge. You and only you are responsible for your drinking.

Am I drinking to repress something?

Repression means to hide or bury painful memories or illogical beliefs. There are so many people who drink because they want to forget someone or to stay away from a painful past. But as we have discussed in the previous chapter, nothing good ever comes from escapism and we can't escape reality. Ask yourself, "Am I drinking to repress my memories or to forget something?" Some memories in our lives are just permanent. Drinking is not a solution, but rather a replacement for a solution. Initially, it might feel that this is a good replacement, but it is too big of a price to pay. No painful memory repression is worth being an alcohol addict. If you know that you are drinking to repress something, mark that as a red flag. Identify the inner pain inside because the pain in your heart cannot be eliminated by alcohol.

Minimizations

I ask a question to many of the people who come to me for counseling. "Can you identify the main problems in your life?" Think about it.

Minimization is the act of making something smaller than it is. The change in the brain chemistry of a drug addict—previously discussed—does not let them decide which event or problem in life matters and which doesn't. Even if you set aside your alcoholism, there are many problems in life that you need to address. For example, money crisis, familial problems, your kids' future, and so on—all these are main issues that need to be addressed. These are the things that matter the most in a person's life. An alcohol addict is reluctant to address these problems. All they want is to have some booze at the end of the day without worrying too much about the real problems. Alcoholics fail to see the bigger picture in life.

When I was a heavy drinker, I couldn't wait for my work hours to end. All I wanted was to get some drinks in at the end of the day. Nothing else really excited me. My wife and my son needed my attention and I needed to give them the love that they deserve. But I minimized the bigger issues in life. That was a red flag.

Projection

Projection is another very common defense mechanism for an alcoholic. This is a way of avoiding responsibility by projecting your own issues onto another person. It can be regarded as blame shifting. Alcoholics may project their own addiction onto others, like a family member who also drinks, for instance. This allows them to not have to think about their own problems. Projection is a means of shifting the spotlight on someone else's negative traits to reduce attention from your addiction. A very common scenario is when a spouse blames the other for their addiction.

The first habit from the *7 Habits of Highly Effective People* by Stephen Covey is being proactive. Most of us are reactive in our lives. Being proactive means to readily recognize one's own deeds and faults. It is the habit of projecting on your own life rather than the lives of others. Projecting others' faults is the opposite of being proactive. In my early days, I have always projected onto my drinking buddies. I took them as my metric and told myself that I was drinking because so were they. What I failed to recognize was my own inability to turn my life around.

Intellectualization

This is a rarer behavior. With the advent of technology and the popularity of social media, misinformation is very common. I would say it is easier to acquire misinformation than facts. People can be exposed to false information. Don't get me wrong. I am not against social media. It can be very useful. But I am against the idea of hurting people by spreading misinformation. So why am I talking about all of this?

This is because intellectualization among addicts is increasing due to the above-mentioned reasons. People are easily led to believe that alcohol is not toxic. All they have to do is use a search engine to do their research. This does not mean that all you read online is misinformation. While most information is accurate, AI can also show you confirmation bias. Don't do your research on social media when it comes to life-and-death situations like alcoholism and alcohol addiction.

Defence mechanisms [4] like the ones mentioned above are all innate behaviors meant to fulfill our desires and avoid facing our faults. These mechanisms help addicts to refrain from self-guilt and the feeling of inadequacy and failure. When using them, a person can develop an inability to deal with their problems or admit their existence. The more defense mechanisms we develop, the more the roots of alcohol addiction will grow. If you are an alcoholic and you are reading this to give up drinking, then you must recognize these red flags right now. Every time the voice in your head suggests you need a drink, ask yourself why'. Then you will be able to identify the defense mechanism in action and you will become more self-aware about your behaviors.

Chapter Summary

Here are the things we learned from this chapter:

- Alcohol content is the right measure of drinking, not how many drinks you have.
- Justifying an ill behavior does not make it any good.
- The more you repress something, the more it persists.
- Be proactive and take responsibility for your own life.
- You can't become an expert when you learn through social media.

In the next chapter you will learn about the physical and mental effects of alcohol.

THREE

The Effects of Alcohol on Health

I KNOW what you are thinking right now. I also know that you understand some facts about how alcohol affects your body and mind. But I want to draw the ultimate picture for you so that you can understand better. The effects of alcohol start slowly but escalate fast. The short- and long-term effects of drinking will change the way you live your life. It will also affect your job performance and relationships with your loved ones. I want you to have a complete idea of what you are doing to yourself. There are so many ill effects of consuming alcohol that an entire book could be written on the subject.

Effects on physical health

Let us begin with the digestive system. If you are a heavy drinker, I'm pretty sure you have felt abdominal cramps, bloating, and gassiness after drinking. I had these symptoms. Even after becoming an alcoholic, sometimes I felt nauseated and even vomited. But the real scenario that goes on inside your stomach and intestines is scarier. Drinking damages the epithelium of the intestinal tract that leads to poor absorption of vitamins and nutrients. Malnutrition becomes highly likely. Epithelial damage may also lead to ulcers which may eventually cause internal bleeding. According to a study, people drinking 50 grams of alcohol—3.5 drinks—per day have 50% higher chances of developing colo-rectal cancer (National Institute of Alcohol Abuse and Alcoholism, n.d.).[1]

Two important organs related with the digestive system are the liver and the pancreas. Alcohol damage to these organs can cause life threatening conditions. The liver is the organ that helps to break down harmful substances from the body, but alcohol interferes with this process. It may also lead to diseases like liver cirrhosis, chronic liver disease, and even liver cancer. Excess drinking can also lead to abnormal activation of pancreatic enzymes (National Centre for Biotechnological Information, n.d.).[2] This may lead to an inflammation of pancreas known as pancreatitis. In fact, chronic consumption of alcohol is the second most common cause of pancreas disease.

Long-term use of alcohol is associated with numerous diseases and conditions. Some heart related problems, including high blood pressure, irregular heartbeat, and heart failure are much more common in alcoholics. Due to damage of intestinal epithelium and lack of absorption of vitamins and minerals, anemia, a condition wherein blood count is low, may also develop (Pietrangelo, n.d.).[3]

Effects on Mental Health

We have already discussed how alcohol affects our brains. Every alcoholic faces mental health issues to some extent after drinking. There are very few alcoholics out there who have not experienced mental symptoms due to their imbibing. Alcohol causes the direct inhibition of the stimulatory neurons in the brain, which results in reduced interaction between the body and the brain. By changing brain chemistry, it causes damage to the central nervous system. This is why it becomes difficult for your brain to create long-term memories. It may also affect your judgement and short-time memory. Alcoholics are very likely to make illogical choices as their cognitive function is suppressed to some extent when drinking.

Heavy drinking is strongly associated with depression, although the exact mechanism is not yet defined. It is assumed that alcohol influences the chemical signals in our brain that are important for mood regulation. Studies have shown that stopping alcohol consumption can improve the mood (Drinkaware, n.d.).[4] I have personal experience with this. Although I started drinking to feel better, I experienced crippling depression when hungover. When I finally stopped drinking, my mood lifted considerably. I felt much happier and enthusiastic when performing my daily activities hangover-free. I am sure if you follow the five methods that I will be teaching in further chapters, you'll experience the same.

The most dangerous effect of alcohol on mental health is that it can lead a person to behave impulsively. An alcoholic in the middle of a drinking binge can harm themselves or even attempt suicide. There is a strong association between chronic alcoholism and suicidal thoughts and attempts. Alcoholics who attempt self-harm when binging are also likely to attempt suicide the longer they go without help.

Effects on reproductive health and fertility

The effects of alcohol on reproductive health are really important. People who want to have children or enjoy a healthy sex life should not be drinking alcohol. Many people drink before initiating sex as alcohol can lower inhibitions and make them more spontaneous. While this is true, the negative effects of drinking are more important.

Men who are heavy drinkers are more likely to face erectile dysfunction in the long run because alcohol inhibits the production of sex hormones. Alcohol may also stop menstrual cycles in women, putting them at great risk for infertility (Pietrangelo, n.d.).[5] Even for people who are not likely to want children in the future, staying healthy is more important than drinking.

Doctors recommend not drinking at all if you are pregnant. Restricting your average intake may prevent complications but there is always risk. The more you drink, the bigger the risk. Regular alcohol consumption also increases the risk of miscarriage. This risk is highest during the first trimester, when the main organs of the fetus are forming. However, drinking alcohol any time during pregnancy can put your baby at risk. The alcohol in the mother's blood can reach the fetus through the placenta and cause massive harm. Fetal alcohol syndrome (FAS) is a condition caused by alcohol consumption during pregnancy that affects the baby's brain. The babies born with FAS have an underdeveloped brain, retarded growth, and other characteristic feature (Pietrangelo, n.d.).[6] This is an example of how your own addiction hurts the people in your life, even your own children.

Here is one of my friend's stories about becoming a mother: *When I decided to have a baby, I read a lot about the effects of alcohol on the developing baby and I was scared. If anything would happen to my first child, I would have nobody but myself to blame and I don't know if I could forgive myself. But by the grace of*

God, I had an amazing partner who has supported me all the way on my journey to stay sober. It was really hard to stay away from alcohol, even knowing it was for such a big purpose. Our baby was okay, and I didn't have to face a nightmare. But that does not mean that it couldn't have happened. Having a baby was the best thing that could have happened to me. Since the birth of my baby, I have not touched alcohol."

My friend was a heavy drinker, just like me. But she never wanted to trade her dream of becoming a mother with alcohol. For her, it was not worth it. It is not worth it for you either.

Effect on social and economic health

This is when you'll have to stay honest with yourself. How many times did alcohol affect your relationships and work? I would guess it happened many times. You can't expect to be a daily drinker and remain 100% efficient at work. If you think you are still at your peak performance, it is just your defense mechanisms kicking in (denial). Job performance, just like your home life, does not improve by drinking alcohol.

The problem with addiction of any kind is that it not only affects the individual, but also the people around them. Your spouse, your kids, your neighbors, your boss, and almost everyone around you is affected by your life choices when you drink. No matter how much you love your kids, if you are spending more time in a bar than at home, they are not going to feel your love. If you are hungover daily, your boss will see the drop in productivity and you may lose your job.

Over the years, I have worked in many places, mostly because I didn't like my co-workers and my boss. I always felt as if everyone was against me, but actually I was the one who was not in the right mind to judge. I was never bad at my job. However, when you spend most of the night drinking, you are probably not at your peak from a cognitive point of view. My co-workers drank too—they were not angels. But they were much more in control and only went out drinking on weekends, unlike me. I was drinking daily.

My home life was a mess too. I thought everything was okay at home, but nothing actually was. My wife and child needed me, but I was not there for them. I wasted all my money on booze. Every father supports their child at sports and school events. Every father except for me, that was. I know now how much I affected all the people I love.

Your drinking can cause mental health issues in your loved ones as well. It can cause fear, anxiety, and depression in your spouse. Many families break up because one spouse is an alcoholic. Is losing the people you love the most worth drinking? I think not. We may have the right to ruin our own lives, but we have no right to ruin the lives and shatter the dreams of our children. It is not acceptable and you should never do it.

If you care about your life, think about the physical and mental health effects and drinking alcohol. If you care about the people around you, you should definitely quit drinking and look to improve your life and your future.

Chapter Summary

Here are the things we learned from this chapter:

- Alcohol affects several important organs of the body including the liver, pancreas, heart, and stomach.
- Alcoholism is highly associated with suicidal thoughts, self-harm, and depression.
- Heavy drinking can markedly affect your sex life and also result in infertility.
- An alcoholic not only harms themselves, but also fails to fulfil their duties towards their loved ones.

In the next chapter, you will learn how to make the decision not to drink.

FOUR

Making the Decision not to Drink

THE FIRST STEP is always difficult, no matter what you do. But when it comes to addiction, the first step seems impossible initially. Over the years, I have counselled thousands of heavy drinkers and they never really wanted me to say, "Make a decision to quit drinking." They wanted me to fix their life without eliminating their drinking habits. That was not possible, obviously, but deep in their hearts they wanted me to say, "You can still lead an amazing life without giving up drinking." I never promised anybody that that was possible. My former drinking buddies would turn white when I told them that they could never be happy without quitting. Making the decision to not drink is a big step that can turn your life around.

The importance of making the decision

Is making a decision that hard? Yes, it is really difficult when you believe in your heart that you can't keep the promise you made to yourself. But it is also important. If you are making the decision to quit drinking, then you are more likely inhibiting the defense mechanisms—the red flags mentioned in Chapter 2—in your brain and that is a good sign. If you are still falling back onto your bad habits, making the decision is not enough but it is a step toward the right direction. Making the right decision at the right time is what makes a good man great. The only way to turn your life around and change your lifestyle completely is to take the first step, making the decision.

As I have mentioned earlier, your alcoholic behaviors not only affect you, but also the people around you. I remember when I made the decision to quit and went to my wife and told her about it. She was so happy that she was almost in tears. She could understand how hard it was for me, but was happy that I was willing to do it because I loved her and our family. Other than your local pub, everyone will be happy to hear you're quitting drinking. How did you feel when you first decided what you wanted to be in your life as a kid? I am pretty sure you felt enthusiastic, encouraged, and excited. I can guarantee that if you have the right mindset, you are going to feel the same. For the first time in many years, you will feel that your life is under your own control. Running your life on autopilot is the last thing you would want in your life. But alcohol and all other addictive substances kick us from the driving seat in our lives. To experience life, you must stay in control. And to stay in control, you need to take the very first step.

Factors that affect your decision

Although taking a decision is solely in your hands, don't expect it to be a smooth path. It is not going to be easy to stick to your decision, and many negative factors will play a role. But there will also be positive factors that will reinforce your decision. For sticking to your decision, you must be resilient and strong. You should always look towards the positive factors and avoid the negative ones. Your family, friends, colleagues, and environment will have a role to play in affecting your decision-making process.

What happens when you tell your drinking buddies that you are quitting after today? Do you expect them to give you a pat on the back? Nope, not at all. They will probably make fun of you and will try to discourage you in every possible way. Your friends do not want to lose your good company, and they also don't want you to lead them in the right direction. This is going to be a setback for you. When I first told my buddies I was quitting drinking, they reacted pretty similarly. They laughed and said, "You've said you'll quit before and here you are." Now, when you make such a big decision and are met with negativity, you are likely to get discouraged. You will start having doubts. The same happened to me. I told myself, "Well, my buddies know me pretty well." But that was not the right way of thinking. At every stage of my life, you should look for the positives. You should always look up to the people that succeed.

The same statement had a completely different reaction at home. My wife, on the brink of tears, told me that she was proud of me. I looked at my children, and for the first time, I felt that I took a step to fulfil my responsibility as a father. My kids were too small to understand what I was doing, but I think if they knew, they would have been happy about it as well. It was one of the best days in our household.

Other than my small family, I also had some friends who supported me. I told these friends what I intended to do, and their reaction was positive. They tried their very best to motivate me and help me stick to my intentions. My drinking buddies were not bad people, but they had their own problem to solve. They couldn't help me and didn't want to. Unfortunately, we had to part ways.

Sealing the decision

When your family and friends help you quit drinking, it becomes a little easier. But nothing compares to your own doubts. When you try to quit drinking, there is always a voice in the back of your head saying, "What if you can't do it?" This voice is a slow poison. It can stay in your head forever, and you can do nothing about it. The best way to fight this voice in your head is to think about how you will be changing your life with just one decision.

The voice kept playing in my head but I kept thinking about my family and friends. I remembered the smile on their face when I told them that I would quit. You do not want to let your loved ones down. But it was not enough, I had to seal the decision once and for all.

Here is what you can do. Take a diary and draw a vertical line in the middle of the page, separating the page into two sections. On the left, list all the things that you gain from drinking. On the right side draw all the things that alcohol has cost you. This is what I did and my right-hand side list got pretty long. On the left side, I only listed two things, "alcohol relaxes my mind and helps me escape problems for the evening." The cons list wouldn't fit on one page, however. Here are some of what I wrote:

- My health
- Money
- Social acceptance
- The job I lost over my drinking
- My family's happiness

- My children's future
- Career progression
- Happiness

There was more, but I think you get the idea. When I looked at the page again and again, I felt guilty and stupid. Everyone says it is not worth it, but that day I acknowledged it.

You should try this exercise right now. It will help you to see visually what an imbalanced trade you are committed to. After reading the list over and over again, my doubts faded away. I could see clearly that whatever I was intending to do was better than what I was already doing. And even if I failed once, twice, or even hundreds of times, I must succeed for all of the reasons on the right side of the page.

Chapter Summary

Here are the things that we have learned from this chapter:

- The first step is difficult but it is essential and liberating.
- Living your life on autopilot is not living at all.
- Only a handful of people really care for your wellbeing. Keep them close.
- Making the decision becomes easier when you can visualize the pros and cons.

In the next chapter, you will learn what you have to change to stick to your decision to quit drinking.

FIVE

What Do You Have to Change?

MAKING the decision to quit is difficult. But you know what is more difficult? Sticking to your decision. You are on the right path if you have taken the decision to quit drinking. Now, the challenge is to stay on the right track and not slip. We make numerous decisions and resolutions every day in our lives, but how many do we actually stick to? Very few, I believe. The reason this happens is because in order to change our habits, we need to change a lot about ourselves. I know this might sound overwhelming and scary. People don't like the idea of change. It is something that scares most of us because change is uncertainty.

Changing your self-image

No, I am not talking about plastic surgery. Changing your identity means changing your self-beliefs. People define their future by their past experiences. They think that if they have failed to stick to a decision in the past, the future will be no different. We all have a self-image that informs us of what we can and cannot do. Most things we think we "cannot do"' come from past experiences. Certain parts of our mind always look back and tell us that the past defines the future. We must realize that this self-image is the result of previous failures which have nothing to do with future success. Just because someone has failed in the past does not necessarily mean that they are never going to be successful in the future. We need to change our self-image.

Your opinions about yourself are widely created by the circumstances and people around you. We have all heard things like, "you are not good enough," "you can never be better," and "your addiction is permanent." These have created lasting impressions in your brain and mind. But it is time to let them go. What you have to remember every now and then is that your past does not define you. You have matured over the years and have become a much stronger individual. You also have the right to define your own future. So, without relying on past experiences or failures, you should pave the path to a new future. The self-image that has limited your potential over the years needs to change.

If humans relied on past experiences of their ancestors and never tried new things, we would never advance as a society. The same goes with your life. You need to forget past failures and impressions and set a mindset for a beautiful future—a future where your self-image does not restrain you but rather liberates you to become the person you want to become.

Shifting your mindset

As Einstein said, "We cannot solve our problems with the same thinking we used when we created them." This quote provides a great deal of insight in problem-solving. You cannot eliminate a problem by remaining in the same mindset. To eliminate a problem or to solve a problem, you need to change your mindset first. You need to take new approaches to the problem. So, how do you change the way you think? Shifting your mindset is not an easy task. The paradigms in your mind have been developing since you were born. But it is not impossible to change them. I realized this when I read *Atomic Habits* by James Clear.[1] It is an amazing book which talks about how we should change the way we think to change a habit. James Clear provides amazing insight into the words we use in our speech that have an impression on our subconscious mind. Let me put this into context.

Let's say that after taking the bold decision of quitting drinking, you were invited to a party. Everyone around you has a glass in their hands and asks you what you'd like to drink. The normal response would be, "I'm trying to stop drinking." But to shift your mindset completely, you need to change your word choices too. Next time anybody asks you about having a drink, your response should be, " Sorry, I don't drink." A person who is trying to stop drinking might fall back into old habits but when you say you don't drink, this is a statement. This simple change of words affects how the brain perceives your decision to not drink. Positive words can force our brain to do good things and vice versa. In the book *Words Can Change Your Brain*, the authors, Newberg and Waldman, mention how the simplest of words can affect our cognitive functions. [2] The simplest change in wording can help encourage your subconscious mind. I am using this technique to this date, not for just staying away from alcohol, but also in many other areas. Whenever I have to do something I don't enjoy, like household chores or dishes, I say to myself, "This is going to be fun." The work does not become more interesting, but the tension and friction is relieved. From the day you have decided that you are going to stop drinking, think of yourself as a non-alcoholic.

Re-writing your relationships

Among all the effects of alcohol, the most common effect that I noticed was how it affects different relationships. If you think of the time before your addiction, your relationship with loved ones was different than it is now. A lot of things have changed. Maybe their perception about you has changed or they don't trust you that much anymore. But whatever the case, the fault was always yours. It is time for you to make up for your past mistakes.

What are the two best things that you can provide to fix your relationship with someone? The answer is attention and time. If you can only provide ample amounts of time and attention to a person, no matter who it is, it will be possible to save a relationship. After taking the decision to quit drinking, I started to pay special attention to my family members. Usually, after work, I wasn't available most nights. But now I am a non-alcoholic who loves to spend time with his family. I try to help my wife with her household chores and my kids with their homework. On weekends, we go on short trips. I try to give them as much attention as possible because I know they are all that matters to me.

If you don't have a family, you still have friends or parents. Give them the time and attention they need. In case you don't have any people in life, we will talk about other replacement habits in the next chapter. Fixing a relationship will take time but it will happen. Many alcoholics said to me, "I have quit drinking but still my family doesn't want me anymore." The answer to this problem is patience. If you feel that your love for them is not helping, the best tip is just to "love them more."

All these changes and improvements don't just apply to alcoholics. Anyone who's unhappy with their life can use them. The sole reason I want people to stop drinking is because it can make them genuinely happy and let them focus on what matters most. If you change your paradigms, shift your mindset, and build healthy relationships with your loved ones, you'll reap the best benefits of quitting.

Chapter Summary

Here are the things we learned in this chapter:

- Get rid of your previous self-image and believe in a better future.
- Choose your words carefully because every word may affect our subconscious mind.
- Fix the relationships that were affected by your ill habits.
- Remember that the end goal of quitting alcohol is to be genuinely happy.

In the next chapter, you will learn how to quit alcohol.

SIX

The First Method—Eliminating the Trigger

IN THE BOOK *Atomic Habits* by James Clear, the author talks about the best ways of giving up on a habit. I have tried all of them, and the one I found most useful was, "make it difficult." In the initial days of quitting drinking, you will be quite motivated and things will work out fine. At least that was the case for me. But as time passed by, my environment presented me with triggers that I was not ready to face. That is when I realized the importance of making it difficult. If you really have the desire to stop drinking, there is no easy way. Before talking about how you can make your drinking difficult, there are some things you need to know about habits.

How does a habit work?

Our lives are a compilation of our habits. Habits are the actions that determine a persons' success. The reason alcoholics are struggling in their lives is because they are the victims of bad habits. The only way to turn your life around is to give up bad habits and work on building good ones. All our habits, good or bad, are formed in a sequence, as per the below diagram.

Cue > Craving > Routine > Reward

The **cue** is the initial trigger or the switch that activates the habit. **Craving** is the innate desire to get the reward. A **routine** is the specific action you perform to get the reward. The **reward** is the end goal of your habit. If you are an alcoholic, your cue is probably your friend's text that invites you to the bar. Craving is the desire you develop the minute you read the text. Routine is the action of drinking, and your reward is the stress-relief or the temporary peace of mind. All the habits that we perform in a day are tied to this cycle one way or another. Knowing the habit pattern will help you to break the cycle easily. You should also keep in mind that it is not possible to alter your craving or reward. So, to break the cycle, you either need to eliminate the cues or change your routine. In this chapter, we will discuss how to eliminate the triggers—cues.

Out of sight, out of mind

Did you ever have an urge to eat pizza after seeing someone else eating pizza on social media or on the street? Of course you have. Maybe you were so tempted that you changed your plans and went to grab a pizza for yourself. If you hadn't been exposed to someone eating pizza, you probably wouldn't have done anything. The same principle can be applied to all of your habits. Getting rid of the cues is the first and foremost thing that you should do. Simple changes in your environment can bring about amazing results. The urge can be suppressed or remain dormant without external triggers. So the best option for you is to get rid of all alcohol in your home.

Simply remove all alcoholic beverages from your home. Also stay away from places that sell alcohol. Keep water and healthy drinks around. If you are living with roommates, ask them to keep drinks in their own rooms. Avoid the beer and wine aisles at the grocery store. They can trigger you to grab a bottle. When I quit drinking, I even avoided watching commercials on TV. I think this helped me a lot. But the most difficult situation I faced during the first fortnight of quitting was a party thrown by one of my colleagues. I couldn't really excuse myself from this party. Everyone was drinking there. The temptation was intense. My boss was there and I was going to ask him for a week off because I wanted to spend some time with my family. So, I put all my focus on what I was going to say to my boss. I realized that when my mind was concentrating on something else, I really couldn't see the drinks anymore. So did I give in to my desires? No, I fulfilled the title of this section; I took the drinks *"out of sight and out of mind."* We'll touch on this again in the next chapter.

The hard way

The path to quitting alcohol is not an easy one. If you care about yourself and your loved ones, be prepared to make some really harsh decisions. You also have to remember that not many people want what's best for you, so don't be influenced by other people. You need to be strong and you have to believe in yourself and your purpose. Criticism is going to be your first enemy. But I believe that if you are true to your cause, criticism will not be a problem.

The first week after I quit, many friends still extended invites that would include drinking. I refused them and tried my best to be polite. Every time they called; the tension rose within me. I will be honest; it was hard to say no because they were really insistent. To an alcoholic trying to quit, a friend insisting that drinks are on them is the siren song. On the weekend, I broke down and accepted an invitation. I figured I'd go to the pub, have a nice chat, and hang out without buying a drink. Well, that's what I thought... When I went inside the pub though, I realized I didn't want to be there to hang out with my friend. What I wanted was to drink and I knew I was going to be able to do it there. I made a quick excuse to my friend, telling him I had an urgent call and left as fast as I could. I would have definitely ended up drinking if I stayed.

Next day I sat down and thought about how I could prevent events like that from happening again. What was the trigger to all this? The phone call. My decision will seem harsh, but I grabbed my phone and blocked all of my former drinking buddies' numbers. Before I did, I texted them one last time, saying, "Hey [friend], as I mentioned many times this week, I am trying to quit drinking for my family. Please do not contact me again." While you may think I acted rudely, I merely responded to them ignoring all my previous statements that I was trying to quit. The fewer toxic people you have in your life, the happier your life is going to be. So I think I made a great choice.

Rid yourself of people like this "friend" of mine. Only surround yourself with those who are genuinely helping you and offering you positive environments to slowly move on from your addiction. Yes, blocking former friends is harsh. However, you have to put your own needs and health first.

Remaining accountable to yourself and your loved ones

As previously mentioned, quitting alcohol is not only a good thing for you but also the people around you. I am sure your friends and family and all the people who really love you will provide you with help. I have seen loved ones go out of their way to help their addicted friends and family. Remember you always have them to share your thoughts and situation with. If you are having trouble coping with your new sobriety, reach out to them.

One of the practices that is really going to help you is accountability. Pick an accountability partner. For me it was my wife, but it can be anyone close to you. Be sure that you are able to share all your thoughts to this person. Whenever you go out, tell your partner where you are going. There are times like I mentioned above when we overestimate ourselves and almost act on our urges. Our accountability partners will help us to point out even the slightest of risks while going somewhere or doing something.

If you don't have someone you can trust, or you just don't want to burden another person with your issues, keep yourself accountable. This is harder than having an accountability partner, however. I put a picture of my family on my phone's wallpaper. This helped to remind me why I am putting myself through all the misery of quitting drinking in the first place. As the phone never left me, I always remained accountable to myself. You will not imagine how this simple change can affect your behavior. You can also journal and remind yourself of why you are doing this. This will reinforce your drive in your subconscious mind. It is likely to create a subconscious hatred of alcohol.

When you stop drinking alcohol, the first weeks are the toughest. You are most vulnerable during this time. A simple trigger can set you off and force you to buy a drink. These tips will help you to remove the initial trigger and surround yourself with positive cues. But remember, you are not flawless. You may even fail to resist the urge during the first few days and drink. Do not be discouraged and do not follow the "all or none law." If you fail, think about the progress you already made. You used to drink every day of the week, but now you stopped after a drink. Give yourself a pat on the back and start again. The only way you are going to fail is if you give up.

Chapter Summary

Things you have learned from this chapter:

- To change a habit, the cue that causes it must be modified or eliminated.
- Optimize your environment to eliminate all triggers.
- Take harsh decisions and go out of your way to give up alcohol.
- Even if you fail, you are still making progress.

In the next chapter you will learn why and how to find replacements for alcohol.

SEVEN

Finding Replacements

HOW DOES a typical day in your life feel like? How often do you think about drinking? How much time do you actually spend drinking? The answer to these questions will make you understand whether alcohol is on your mind a lot every day. In the earlier chapters we have talked about how to change your thinking and how to act right after you quit, but what do you do next? When you quit drinking, a huge void is created that needs to be filled again.

In my experience, initially I felt hollow inside. My mind would feel like I needed to do something, but I could not really figure out what.

Choosing a new favorite

If an empty bottle is kept empty for too long, it probably needs to be thrown out. Quitting left a hole in your life that you need to fill again. The first thing that you need to do is choose a new favorite drink. I know this might sound weird but there will be instances when this will be really useful.

During my second week of sobriety, I went to a restaurant with my family. I was supposed to order a drink. Obviously, I wasn't going to drink alcohol. However, I found myself looking at the bar. My wife, also my accountability partner, saw this and gently reminded me that I should look at the soft drinks instead. I took her advice and ordered some pretty good lemonade. From that day onwards, this has become my drink of choice. This means that I always have a glass in my hand just like other people, so I don't feel so left out.

When it comes to filling up this void, there is more to it than just your favorite drink. Let's talk about your favorite place to hang out. As an alcoholic, it was probably a bar or pub. To get out of the toxic bubble of your past, you need to find a better place to hang out. You can't be in a place that triggers you. Find your special place. Try out different places every week and see what you like the best. Make sure to avoid places which sell or promote alcohol.

You have changed your drink and your place, what is the one thing that is missing? Yes, the people. In the previous chapter I have already mentioned why and how you should avoid your drinking buddies. Now it is time for you to hang out with new people. You don't need to make new friends and acquaintances. You just need to avoid people that trigger you to drink and return to your old ways. This will help you to fill up the lack of social interaction.

A new hobby

Replacing things is great. But is it enough to replace a bad habit? No, all habits come about for a reason. You didn't drink alcohol because it tasted good but because of how it alleviated your stress or prevented you from thinking about your problems. Your new favorite drink will help you avoid drinking again but what about the stress and anxiety? These feelings don't go away by themselves. You need to find another way of dealing with anxiety and depression. Earlier in this book we talked about how we can only change the trigger and routine but never the reward and urge. The best way to get rid of a habit is to replace it with another habit that gives you similar rewards but does not harm you as much.[1]

Think about the things that excite you. Football, gardening, video games, exercising—it could be anything you want. If you cannot find one, then try some and see what works. You need to channel your focus on a hobby you enjoy. After a hard day at work, you cannot just sit around and expect all the stress to just go away. Maybe you can sit down and watch a show on Netflix with your family. If you are single, then maybe you can try playing games with your friends. You can even try to make your own Youtube channel or a blog. These will keep you busy and keep you from thinking about drinking. If you are able to find something that you are truly interested in, you'll be stress-free more easily. For me, playing video games was the way out. Some games were really immersive. After two weeks of playing my favorite game, I wasn't thinking about drinking after work anymore.

Many of my friends adopted pets when they quit drinking. This helped them get out of the house and avoid thinking about drinking. They also got emotionally attached to their pets. Instead of spending nights at the pub drinking, they'd go for a walk around the neighborhood with their new buddies or take them to the dog park. This became their hobby. Anything that you love and which doesn't involve alcohol can help here.

Changing your schedule

Everyone has a schedule in their lives; it is written or in their minds and it is very difficult to change once you get used to it.

My own schedule looked sort of like this: wake up, go to work, come back from work, go to the pub, get drunk, come home late, pass out, and repeat. If you look at your schedule, you probably also have a steady routine that also involves heavy drinking at some point during the day. When you quit, this is the time when you may feel the most vulnerable to thinking about drinking. So you need to tidy up your schedule and stay busy during this time every day.

Here is what I did. When I went home from work, I concentrated on my kids and wife. I tried helping my kids with their homework. After 8.30 p.m., which was the time I usually went out to drink, I scheduled an activity every day. I was never free at that time. I always had something to do. I was not allowed to make excuses. I'd wash the car, clean the yard, or clean inside the house. This was all in my schedule. I planned each week in advance.

Here is what I want you to do. Sit down with a piece of paper and write down some of the important chores or activities that you always leave to your spouse or you need to do yourself. These don't all have to be chores. They can also be enjoyable things. Plan an entire week and schedule them around the time you used to start drinking. This particular activity will help you stop thinking about drinking at that time. Stay focused on whatever activity you select. The more you let yourself get bored, the easier it will be for the urge to come back. The busier you are, the less you'll think about taking up drinking again.

The key idea of finding a replacement is to forget that you are missing something in life. If you stop using alcohol, then something else should fill up this empty space that it left in your life. The more you enjoy the new hobby, the more you separate yourself from the previous version of yourself. During the first weeks after quitting, it might seem impossible to stay away from alcohol. But a change of scenery can change your outlook. These replacements will help to strengthen your belief in your new identity, as a non-alcoholic.

Chapter Summary

Here is what we have learned from this chapter:

- The best way to change a bad habit is to replace it with a good one.
- Picking a new favorite drink, a favorite place to go, and new friends will help you to forget your addiction.
- There are better ways of eliminating your stress and anxiety than alcohol.

In the next chapter you will learn about the 24-hour program and how we can take baby steps to achieving our goals.

EIGHT

The 24-Hour Plan

YOU MUST BE WONDERING how I managed to quit alcohol on my first try. Well, the real scenario is a little different. When I was still drinking, I'd often think about quitting. When I first got married, when my first child was born, and so many other times I told myself that I was done with drinking. I was determined that this time it would work. I had done research and was completely motivated. But after the first couple of weeks, I fell back into the same patterns. I considered starting drinking again and thought I'd try quitting after a month or a year. I'm pretty sure you can relate to this. We all know how alcohol can harm us in many ways and we all have tried to quit. But unfortunately, the urge is too strong to resist and the pledge to quit is too big to keep. So how did I manage to quit drinking for good this time?

The 24-hour plan

We cannot expect to change our life in just one day. If it was that easy, then everyone would do it. The reason it is so hard makes it more worth it. The best way to approach life is to take baby steps instead of big leaps. If you improve even a little bit every day, at the end of the year you would be a lot better. Maybe the first day seems insignificant but when you add the days, you'll see great results. The 24-hour plan is a solid plan to take small steps towards staying sober.

The 24-hour plan does not encourage us to make big pledges or promises to ourselves or our loved ones. Rather than focusing on the longer term, this plan is focused on the next 24 hours. Thinking too far ahead in the future is unproductive. We never know what the future holds. The best way to control our life is to control the present. Your focus should be entirely on how you can avoid drinking for the next 24 hours. When you wake up in the morning the one affirmation you should say to yourself is "Not today." It is a much more realistic approach than quitting drinking forever. Sometimes, when the urge starts kicking in, you can even break down the 24 hours into smaller parts, even down to one hour. You can just tell yourself, "Not this hour." Use the hobbies we discussed in the last chapter. You'll realize that the urge is not as strong when the hour has passed. It's not easy, but it works.

Why the plan works

Most alcoholics are shocked when you tell them to quit drinking forever. But if you tell them to avoid drinking for the next 24 hours, they will say it is doable. This is because it *is* doable. Your mind plays a great role in this type of behavior. When you provide it with a realistic objective it is much likely to fulfil it. Have you ever tried jumping down from the sixth step of the stairs? It is not entirely impossible but it is overwhelming and scary. You can even get hurt. Think about video games. Do you get to defeat the toughest boss first? No, the difficulty slowly increases and you adapt to it. The 24-hour program is quite similar to this. It focuses on taking one step at a time rather than jumping down from the middle of the stairs. Although the end goal is the same, it tricks your brain into thinking "this is easy and I can do this." When you actually remain sober for 24 hours, you complete a small goal. Completing a goal is always fulfilling. It will inspire you for the next day. These small wins everyday will add up in the end.

When you say that you'll never drink again it's tough to achieve such a feat by comparison to taking the 24-hour approach. Completing even the smallest pledges feels good and rewarding. It will make you feel empowered and in control. You are likely to feel the positive reinforcement within you. The satisfaction gained from this small win will make you believe that you can do it again tomorrow. You will start to realize that staying sober for a week or even a month is not that tough.

Avoiding the "all or nothing" law

If you can't do it right, you might as well give up. This is the "all or nothing" law. Many heavy drinkers quit and stay sober for a while, then end up drinking again. This is when this law kicks in. I have heard many alcoholics say, "I lasted two weeks and then I drank again. I failed, so I might as well keep drinking." This can happen to you too. If you slip and drink after being sober for a while, it's an accident, not a failure. Going back to drinking is the failure.

The 24-hour program helps you to measure your success or failure in the context of a day. You don't have to think about what you did yesterday or last week. Only focus on today. If you can avoid drinking for 24 hours, your day is a success. Even if you drank yesterday, it does not affect the success of today. This program gives you a chance to win every single day or even to win every hour. You are always one drink away from a successful or unsuccessful day. When you start thinking like this, you avoid the all or nothing, black and white mindset. When I first found out about this idea, I was skeptical. But as I started doing it, I realized that it's the best way to avoid drinking or thinking about it. In no time, I realized that by avoiding alcohol for one day at a time, I had spent over a month not drinking.

Tracking the small wins

After about a month of sobriety, I got a lot of stress at work. I felt the urge to have a small drink again. That is when my accountability partner, my wife, showed me the calendar she kept for me. I was 32 days sober! She had been crossing out each day of success for me. To be honest, I really wanted a drink. However, seeing those days crossed out like that stopped me. I wanted the streak to continue. I couldn't bring myself to break it. It just didn't feel good. I didn't make myself a drink that night. When you can see your streak of success, you just want to keep winning. Nobody likes to lose. They want to keep going as far as they can for as long as they can.

After every 24 hours of sobriety, cross out the day on a calendar. It will feel good, I can assure you! It will also help to motivate you for the next day. After a week or a fortnight it will feel even better when you see all those dates crossed out. If you are like me, you would like to take positive reinforcement to the next level. I posted my 60-day streak of quitting alcohol on my Facebook profile. The post blew up with comments congratulating me. I started to feel that all the small wins of 24 hours led to me this great win of two months. Tracking your success will not only help you to stay away from alcohol but also make you feel good about yourself.

Big leaps are combinations of small steps. If you want to remain sober for the next five years, start by staying sober for the next 24 hours. Take baby steps because even the tiniest changes in our lives can bring massive results. The 24-hour program will help you to build self confidence that will not only help you to avoid drinking but also improve other aspects of your life. It will increase your self-awareness and mindfulness to enjoy the present without worrying about your past and the future.

Chapter Summary

Here is what we learned from this chapter:

- The best way to approach self-development is by improving 1% every day.
- All you need to do is avoid having a drink.
- Seeing your progress can help you stay motivated.
- All big leaps start with small steps.

In the next chapter you will learn about medications and supplements that will help you stop drinking.

NINE

When the Going Gets Tough

WITH THE RIGHT mindset and great replacements available, it is possible to get rid of your alcohol habits for good. But for some people this is not enough. When people are too deeply involved in their habits, it is not easy to change their behavior or find replacements. Maybe you will find the right mindset, but every now and then your inner voice will still get you to think about drinking.

Maybe you will find your new favorite drink, your new place to be but you still think fondly of the pub you used to drink your favorite alcoholic beverage. Maybe you will use the 24-hour program, but you constantly put off quitting to drink until the next day. You can always fall back on your coping mechanisms, including drinking.

Although you should be done with drinking by using the previous methods described in this book, it doesn't always work. If you can't seem to move beyond drinking using these methods, medication might be right for you. I know you might feel skeptical about this. I was too. But that is why I want to discuss how these medications work and how they can help you to give up alcohol. Remember, if you are just starting out, you don't need the medications. You should try the lifestyle changes first, then move on to the harder steps. **All drugs mentioned below must be tried under the supervision of your doctor.**

Taking drugs to control your alcoholism is a big step to take. Most of these medications are going to prevent the "feel good" part of drinking. We are also going to discuss side effects for each drug. Three drugs have FDA approval for alcohol use disorder and they all work in different ways.

Disulfiram

This is the first drug which was approved by the FDA for alcoholism. Disulfiram is also known as Antabuse and it changes the metabolism of alcohol in your liver. The enzymes which are responsible for breaking down alcohol are deactivated so you get sick every time you have a drink (WebMD, n.d.).[1] Because of this, people are likely to avoid drinking alcohol. Rather than giving them a pleasant experience, the drug gives them an experience that they would like to forget. Disulfiram is for people who are determined and are firmly motivated to quit, but have failed, nevertheless. It can also be used by people who have gotten an ultimatum from their family or work.

If you drink while on disulfiram, you'll experience nausea, vomiting, sweating, headaches, and a really unpleasant feeling of anxiety. The most common problem with disulfiram is that alcoholics usually stop taking the drug rather than quitting drinking. I have witnessed this myself. But you can take it when you feel particularly triggered or when you feel depressed and can sense that your urge to drink is taking hold. If you already know that you are going to feel really bad after having a drink, you are most likely to avoid it. The whole objective of using this drug is to create aversion to drinking, making it a dreadful experience rather than a pleasant one.

Naltrexone

The trade name of Naltrexone is ReVia. An injectable form named Vivitrol is also available. This drug was first developed for treating opioid addiction. In the 1980s, it was also discovered that it helped reduce alcohol consumption. Research showed that if naltrexone is combined with psychosocial therapy, it can decrease relapse rates and help in diminishing alcohol cravings (WebMD, n.d.).[2] This drug works by inhibiting the reward pathway in the brain that we discussed earlier. When you drink after taking naltrexone you don't feel the pleasure you were supposed to feel. All the pleasant effects of alcohol are eliminated. The medication can help in reducing your urge to drink as well. When you have an alcohol problem, thinking about alcohol can trigger a pleasurable response. Naltrexone can prevent the association between pleasure and alcohol.

Just like any other drug, you can expect some side effects of Naltrexone. Some common symptoms include stomach cramping, restlessness, trouble sleeping, nausea, and headache. Although they are common side effects, if they seem to persist for too long, you should consult your doctor. Also, if symptoms like rash, blurred vision, itching, hallucination, and depression occur, see your doctor immediately (Mayoclinic, n.d.).[3]

Acamprosate

Acamprosate is the latest medication approved for the treatment of alcoholism in the U.S. It has been widely used in Europe for a long time. This medication works by interfering with two neurotransmitters in the brain, GABA and glutamate. It ensures the balance of these neurotransmitters to reduce the discomfort or withdrawal symptoms from quitting alcohol. It was mainly designed for stabilizing the brain (WebMD, n.d.).[4] As we mentioned earlier, alcohol changes brain chemistry which leads to decreased cognitive function. Acamprosate helps prevent this and improve the memory and cognitive function in affected individuals.

Some side effects of this drug include diarrhea, gas, loss of appetite, and nausea. Serious side effects include rashes and burning or tingling sensations in your limbs.

The role of the physician

This is a story about Samuel, a young man I used to know. Samuel was a young adult, about 21 years old, and a heavy drinker. He was desperate to stop drinking because his girlfriend had threatened to leave him if he did not. When he heard that I stopped drinking, he came to my house one day for counseling. I told him to take it slow and focus on changing his mindset and on finding good replacements. But as I said, he was desperate and he wanted a shortcut. So he went back to his house and researched medications on his own. He didn't bother to call a doctor because he thought he had all the information he needed. After six weeks of taking medication, he was very sick. Later he was diagnosed with hepatitis (National Center for Biotechnological Information, n.d.).[5] Although he did not drink, taking drugs unsupervised had gotten him really sick. This happened because he had a prior chronic hepatitis C infection. He should have never been given the medication without a prior doctor visit and a prescription. Luckily, he survived. The reason I am mentioning this story is to highlight that no matter what you research on your own and how much you trust your sources, you should always consult a doctor before making decisions about taking drugs.

I wanted you to be aware of these medications and what they do. But that doesn't in any way mean that you can prescribe medications for yourself. I didn't make up Samuel's story. It was real and he was lucky to not die because of his mistake. Only your doctor can give you a proper insight about different drugs and how to use them correctly. When you are an alcoholic, you should try to use all the help you can get because you cannot win this fight alone. Also immediately consult your doctor if you're experiencing side effects while on these medications.

When I came to know that different medications can help me change my habits, I was desperate to try them too. I thought that was the easy way out but I was wrong. Alcoholics should only use drugs when they feel that resisting the urge is becoming too hard for them. Most of the people I counseled felt that drugs are a last resort. That's because, without lifestyle and mentality shifts, medications can only help you temporarily. Take all the time you need to adapt to your new life as a non-alcoholic. I would recommend you, time and again, not to be hasty because your craving for alcohol is not something that can magically disappear within a month. You have developed this bad habit for months or even years, so it will take a long time to condition yourself out of it. Be patient because good things only happen to those who wait.

The withdrawal symptoms

Now that you understand medications, their effects, and brain chemistry, you should also learn about withdrawal symptoms. If you are a heavy drinker, I am sure you have heard about this term. Even if you don't, you have surely experienced this. An alcoholic who has been drinking for weeks, months, or years can face some serious symptoms after quitting alcohol. These symptoms are known as withdrawal symptoms.

These symptoms occur after a heavy drinker stops drinking abruptly. They occur in the following order:

- after 6 hours, you can experience anxiety, tremors, headache, nausea, insomnia
- after 12-48 hours, you can experience hallucinations and seizures
- after 48-72 you can experience severe symptoms of vivid hallucinations and delusions, palpitations, fever, and high blood pressure [6]

When you drink alcohol for several months or years, your brain becomes used to it. The brain chemistry changes and the absence of alcohol cause the above-mentioned symptoms. They are unpleasant enough that many people continue drinking so that they don't have to experience them. Not everyone develops serious symptoms. Whenever you face any withdrawal symptoms, consult your doctor. They will be able to diagnose the exact problem. Usually, if it is not a serious health condition, a supportive environment and treatment is all you need to treat alcohol withdrawal. In case your condition is serious, you may be prescribed medication by your doctor.

Withdrawal symptoms are obstacles that most alcoholics face during their recovery. It is absolutely essential to know what symptoms you can develop and also to notify your doctor beforehand that you quit drinking. Your doctor can keep an eye on you and your health as you detox. Also, let your doctor know the complete history of your addiction and any other illness you may have. This information can play a vital role in selecting the ideal treatment for you.

When you quit drinking, every once in a while, you are going to feel that having a drink is the easy way out. Don't pour that drink. You have to endure the pain today to spare it in the future. The withdrawal symptoms can be conquered. You will feel better. Believe in yourself and never give up because you have come very far.

Chapter Summary

Here is what we learned from this chapter:

- If you fail to quit drinking with the help of mind shift changes or the 24-hour program, there is always the option to take medications.
- Every drug has side effects. Never take drugs that were not prescribed by a doctor.
- Withdrawal symptoms are signs that you are heading the right way. Stay strong and inform your doctor that you quit drinking and are going through withdrawal.
- Always let your doctor know about symptoms you experience when you're going through withdrawal.

In the next chapter you will learn the most difficult, yet the most effective step to give up alcohol.

TEN

The Most Difficult Step

BY NOW YOU know almost everything you need to know about giving up alcohol for good. But the stress, anxiety, and life issues are not going to go away if you do not let them go yourself. Many people succeed in giving up alcohol on their first try, but relapse as they fail to deal with the realities of their life. If you are going to relapse after one or two years, all the hard work you've put in will be in vain. At the beginning of this book, I told you that if you apply what you learn here and are honest about it, you can stop drinking in six months. But I would also like to add that if you take this very last step, in the right direction, your chances of relapse will diminish to 10%. So what is this last difficult step? It is *visiting a psychotherapist*.

Why do you need a therapist?

"Robert, I am already doing all I can and I am also making progress. Why do I need a therapist?" This is the first response I get from everyone when I tell them to see a therapist. If your daily life is going steady, you will feel that the four steps mentioned are quite enough. But every now and then, you'll experience some issues. You can't anticipate it, but there will be troubles in your life that will put you under immense stress and anxiety. Your habits will be affected by these circumstances in your life. That is when it will be hard to prevent relapse. The main objective of talking to a therapist is to diminish your suppressed desire to drink once and for all. A therapist can help you to alleviate your inner insecurities and help you relieve stress.

I know what you are thinking after reading that. You're all set. You have your accountability partner who can be your spouse, your best friend, or someone you truly trust. Why do you need to talk to some stranger about all this? Well, let's see why. First off, you are going to talk to a stranger exactly because this person is a stranger. The therapist is not going to judge you for what you are or what you might feel. What if the very root cause of all your problems is your wife or your best friend? What if these people become tired of your troubles because of what is going on in their lives? What if they push you away?

A therapist will not push you away, nor will they get tired of your troubles. That's their job and they are pretty good at it. I'm not saying you shouldn't share things with your partner or your best friend, but I'm suggesting that you need to speak about things you wouldn't share with even those people whom you love and trust. A therapist will not judge you for who you were or who you are. For this person, you are just another patient who needs help. A therapist is solely looking to help you.

I was also having doubts about visiting a therapist just like you. I reluctantly went to one and did not expect much to come out of it. But eventually I started to feel how it changed different aspects of my life, not only my drinking habits. I later realized that you can only feel the importance of something when you actually experience it firsthand. So, why not give everything a try?

Is it difficult? Why?

Based on your personality, you might find it really difficult to see the therapist or you may not. I've been advising people to see a therapist for a long time. Some immediately looked for an available therapist and made an appointment. But others were doubtful and were not open to the idea. Even when I convinced them to see a therapist, they really did not believe that the prospect would work out. One of the key lessons in life that I have learnt is that you can only change a behavior, habit, or yourself if you have firm belief in the process. We have talked about this in the earlier chapters but I can't stress enough how important it is for you to trust the process of psychotherapy. Again, I advise against researching whether psychotherapy is effective or not on the internet. You're likely going to get reinforcing bias by doing so. You are just going to be more reluctant to make an appointment. To give you an idea, about 75% of people who enter psychotherapy gain some sort of benefit from it. (American Psychiatric Association, n.d.)[1]

When going to therapy, some people encounter another issue, namely talking about things that are very personal and intimate to them. I have been in your shoes and I felt the same. I had a number of secrets, realizations, insecurities, and issues that I didn't share with anybody. How can I just talk about these with someone I've just met? This question kept ringing through my head. I know the same thing is happening to you as you read this. You might be a really shy or guarded person who doesn't like to share anything with anyone about your personal affairs. There are millions of reasons why it is difficult for someone to talk to a therapist. Some people try for a couple of weeks and then give up because it doesn't seem to work. But in reality, they just don't want to feel vulnerable. The fear of being vulnerable is what holds most people off. "I am making progress. I can do this without a therapist. I am good on my own. What's the therapist going to say, anyway?" These are some voices that can arise in our heads when we defend why we don't need therapy. They arise from the same defense mechanisms as our need to drink.

Finding the right therapist

This is an important step. When you agree to talk to a therapist, people you know and trust are going to come up with many recommendations. I would suggest you try more than one recommendation because there are many types of professionals out there. Each one of them has a different approach. Some might use harsher methods, some might be too friendly for your liking, and some might not understand you well enough. It is solely up to you as to what you prefer. But don't give up if the first few therapists don't work out. Keep asking for recommendations. Ask your doctor if they have a therapist they trust and recommend. Seeing a therapist will not only help you to alleviate the drinking problem but also help you to diminish your daily stress and anxiety. Once you find the therapist that works for you, open up and tell them all you can about yourself.

How to open up during therapy

It can feel scary to share anything with your therapist during the first few weeks of therapy, especially for introverts. You might be worried about what the therapist is thinking about you. You may worry that you are annoying or you are saying things that you weren't supposed to say or that are inappropriate. Similar thoughts went through my head when I went to therapy for the first time. That is why it is really important to find a therapist who is suitable for you. You don't have to tell them everything during your first session. Take it slow and try to get comfortable first. You don't have to know all about your therapist but at least it is better to talk to an acquaintance than a complete stranger. If you are not comfortable, you won't be able to talk openly with them.

We have talked about all the reasons why a person gets addicted in the first place. Remember, all those reasons are what stops you from having the life you always wanted. These secrets, pain, anxieties, and insecurities haunt you and affect your mental health because you keep them separated from the rest of our lives. They occupy a huge portion in your mind that makes you feel that you are not good enough for anything and you are unworthy. You cannot run away from these thoughts and emotions. They live with you forever. The only way they can be minimized is when you share these with someone. While your friends and family may not always have time to listen to your issues, a therapist is paid to do so. And this person is probably the only one that can help you to get rid of all your suppressed emotions. Opening up in front of a stranger is not an easy task, but if it helps you make your life better, why not give it a try? Sometimes, all a person needs is someone's attention. People need someone who can listen to all their problems. This is especially applicable for addicts who probably got derailed from their goals because of lack of attention and care. A therapist will give you the necessary attention and mental support that you might not find anywhere else. When you are quitting such a habit as hard to beat as alcoholism, you are at your most vulnerable. A therapist can help you to build strength and keep going.

Seeing a psychotherapist is the most difficult of the five steps we've discussed because, in this case, you need to come out of your bubble. You need to leave your comfort zone and talk about your life with someone that you barely know. Psychotherapy along with medication has proven to be greatly effective in preventing both alcoholism and relapse. It had a tremendous effect in my life too. You will never know how much a therapist can help you until you actually give it a try. Give it a shot! You have changed your mindset, found replacements, followed the 24-hour program, taken medications, and now you're in therapy. You have come a long way and are headed in the right direction! Taking this last final step will help you to forget the urge and need for alcohol forever.

Chapter Summary

Here is what we learned from this chapter:

- A psychotherapist can help you to minimize the need for alcohol and reduce the chances of relapse.
- Opening up to an unknown person can be difficult, but it is worth it.
- All your insecurities are holding you off from reaching your potential.
- The only way to minimize your problems is to share them.

In the next chapter you will learn how your future might change if you stop drinking alcohol forever.

ELEVEN

The Life of Your Dreams

STARTING WHEN WE WERE CHILDREN, we've been cultivating some unrealistic dreams in our lives. Maybe it was being a famous celebrity, living in a huge mansion, or being a best-selling author. When you start growing up, you start to realize how absurd some of those dreams were. Most people don't hold on to their childhood dreams; rather, they develop realistic dreams and expectations for their lives. No matter what your dreams are, what you truly want in life is to be genuinely happy. The reason you wanted to attend a Katy Perry concert when you were a kid, for example, is because you liked her songs and they made you feel joy. You wanted to become a great author because you loved writing and it made you feel like you had meaning in life.

We chase happiness throughout our lives, not noticing that happiness resides within all of us. I am writing this book because I have wasted many years of my life searching for happiness. I didn't realize that I was the one pushing it away. I want the readers to know that they can have a far better life only if they commit to quitting drinking forever. Alcohol and all addictions are a vicious cycle that pulls you away from happiness and inner peace. If you are an alcoholic who comes home at midnight and spends the next whole day thinking about their next drink, you are not actually living your life; you are just existing. Just changing this one single habit can change the course of your life. As we have shown, your family is also affected by this habit that you maintain.

Benefits to physical health

We have already talked about how alcohol could harm you. But what changes can you expect when you stop drinking alcohol for a while? When you drink too much, you get what is called an alcoholic face which is used to describe the negative effects of alcohol on your skin. But after quitting alcohol for some time, your skin gradually restores its elasticity and discoloration of skin slowly disappears alongside puffiness.

Alcohol is also closely associated with sleep disorders. Think about it for a second. After a night of heavy drinking, how often have you felt hungover in the morning? Quite a lot, I would assume. When you're hungover, your productivity decreases both in work and school. This happens because alcohol interferes with the sleep cycle and may even cause sleep apnea and snoring (Very well Mind, n.d.).[1] Although at the beginning of alcohol detox you may face some troubles falling or staying asleep due to withdrawal symptoms, gradually your sleep quality will improve and you will be refreshed in the morning.

Alcohol also interferes with the metabolism and absorption of the nutrients in the body (Very well Mind, n.d.).[2] It deprives the body of essential nutrients leading to malnutrition. This malnutrition may lead to numerous other diseases, which could be fatal. Quitting alcohol will help you to regain your nutrition and help you gain or lose weight. It will provide you with the essential nutrients and will protect your body from infection and disease.

From my personal experience, I could feel changes in my body for the better after the first two months of being sober. It was pretty obvious because my energy levels increased tenfold. I could work more and never felt tired or sluggish anymore. I felt as if I was reborn because it was an unnatural amount of energy that I didn't expect. The mornings were more refreshing and even after a stressful day I had enough energy to do household chores and help my family.

Benefits to mental health

According to the National Survey on Drug Use and Health, 9.2 million American adults faced mental illnesses and substance use disorders in 2018 (Substance Abuse and Mental Health, n.d.,).[3] Mental health is closely tied with alcoholism because of the changes in brain chemistry previously mentioned in this book. As you start your alcohol detox, you will start to feel an improvement in your mental health. This includes increased self-confidence and self-respect. Not only that, but you will also start to feel more positive and find it easier to deal with anxiety and stress. Therapy will also help alleviate anxiety and allow you to move away from past failures. When you take a huge step towards living your best life, such as quitting drinking, you really feel great about yourself.

I remember how my perception about everything changed when I stopped drinking. I used to blame my circumstances, my situation, or someone else for everything that went wrong with me, including drinking. But I learnt to take responsibility for myself and my choices. I developed self-respect because I believed that if I could come out of this heinous cycle of abuse, I can do anything. The overthinking and constant blame was no longer there. It was as if I was able to suddenly think more clearly than before. My mind and brain felt liberated.

Benefits to social life and relationships

This is the aspect I was most happy with. My family could feel what I was going through. They developed immense respect for me because of what I had done. It was so pleasing because that is all I wanted, to become a good father and a good husband. I became the role model of my family. My wider circle of friends and acquaintances were also proud of my achievement. It felt good. I also felt that it was far easier to build relationships when I was sober than when I was drunk all the time.

When you stop drinking for a few months, your cognitive functions start to improve. This plays a great role in building and maintaining relationships. You can also spend more time with your friends and family because you're not chasing booze all the time.

Before I quit, hanging out with people was all about drinking. But now I realize how delusional I really was. I get to spend so many weekends trying out exciting new adventures with my friends and family. I'm able to give my time and attention to the people who need it and deserve it. My relationships with colleagues and my boss improved. I am no longer the employee who is late on most days and shows up to work with a hangover and blood-shot eyes. I can now focus on being productive at work and being a family man at home. This new version of me that was within me but I never could realize when I was drinking is amazing!

Alcohol is holding you back from the life of your dreams. You should know that there is much more to see and do in life than binge-drinking at the pub. I'm telling you all this because it is true and I have experienced it firsthand. You deserve all the happiness in the world. I am not saying quitting alcohol is going to get rid of all of your problems, but it is the first step in the right direction. Problems are still going to be a part of life, but if you are an alcoholic, you will never have the guts to face them. I have heard people say, "I don't want a good life for myself." I hope people who feel this way read this chapter and rethink their attitude. Aren't these benefits a thousand times better than the life you are living now, as an alcoholic? The question is rhetorical.

Chapter Summary

Here is what we learned from this chapter:

- Your end goal is to become genuinely happy. Keep that in mind.
- Alcohol detox will give your body and mind better coordination and provide you with a boost of energy every day.
- Quitting alcohol will provide you the time and will to build the relationships that actually matter in your life.

Afterword

You were halfway through your process to rid yourself of alcohol when you picked up this book for the first time. By now you know all about alcohol, how it works, how it affects every facet of your life and health, and all the practical life experiences ruins. I have tried to draw the picture time and again of how low a person can fall because of this single bad habit. Nobody is a loser in their life until they allow themselves to be one. Staying trapped in the vicious cycle of alcohol consumption and abuse is no better than chasing an illusion for the rest of your life. Why would you like to end up like Jean, whom we introduced in Chapter 1?

Before reading this book, you probably have never given a thought about why you need to drink in the first place. You never really thought about how you are unconsciously defending your behavior. But if you are not aware of how your own mind works, you will never be able to control it and change your ways. Quitting alcohol requires more than just some tips and tricks. It requires a complete change in mindset and perspective. This is why making the decision to quit was so tough. You were not only making a decision to quit alcohol, you were making a decision to change who you are. The change in your mindset, your self-image, and your relationships is essential for the five steps to take effect.

All of the five steps complement each other in a very smooth fashion. Your whole alcohol detox can sit on these five pillars. Here's a final look at the five steps that can give you your life back.

1. Remove anything that triggers you to drink.
2. Find replacements to alcohol that are not addictive.
3. Always avoid the "next drink."
4. If you're struggling with the previous steps, visit your doctor to learn more about available medication.
5. Request a therapist referral.

It is easier said than done. But I have faced all of these in my life, so I can guarantee you that they are both doable, and with the right mindset, they are comparatively easier than what you expect. However, one of the first things that you require to change your alcohol abuse is to gain acceptance and believe in yourself. Do not be skeptical about it. If you have finished reading this book, I am sure that you honestly and strongly want to give up alcohol. But many things around you will demotivate you in this quest. I want you to be strong like a rock and follow my advice for at least six months.

People drink for various reasons, none of them happy ones. They drink because they are stressed, have been traumatized, or cannot deal with the bigger issues in their lives. Some people try to quit and fail. But the truth is, you only fail when you yourself say you failed. The way I see it, there is no failure, just progress. Each of the five steps mentioned in this book is a step forward to a better life and a better version of yourself. Starting with the decision to see a psychotherapist, it is a rocky journey. But it is a journey that must be continued for your own benefit and for the sake of your family and friends. You need to let go of all the older versions of yourself and try to build yourself from the ashes as a new and a better version of yourself. Both you and your loved ones deserve a better life than what you have. You just have to try a little bit harder.

A great life is waiting out there for you and you need to make a good choice. The choice is between life or death, happiness or pain and misery, and between being in loving relationships and being lonely. You know that at the end of the day, you don't want to choose drinking over all that is important and dear to you. The choice is pretty obvious, but some people fail to get it right. I have written this book for the sole purpose of helping you to change your fate. I don't want you or anyone to face what I've faced as an alcoholic.

Destruction is imminent when you're addicted. Just when you think everything is going well, it can take everything away from you. You can't let your life become the nightmare of addiction and loss. This book can be your guide at all times. It is appropriate for all ages. You can even just read the key takeaways to save time. Whenever you feel demotivated or discouraged, I would recommend you read a part of this book so that you can understand that the difficulties you are facing are temporary.

Along with all other alcoholics, I have faced the same tribulations while recovering. It was tough and I didn't think I was going to succeed. However, I'm here to tell you that they will go away and you will see the face of a new, brighter dawn. I never promised that it would be easy to give up alcohol but I can guarantee that it will be worth it. I promised at the beginning of this book that if you strictly follow these five steps in the next six months, you will be able to break the chains of addiction forever. I stick to my words. Don't hesitate, take the leap of faith. You only miss this chance if you don't take it.

I want to wish the best of luck to anyone reading this. I have tried my best to offer you my own experience as a way to prevent you from going through the hell I did. I sincerely hope that it helps you in your life now and forever. Enjoy your new, alcohol-free life!

Bibliography

Introduction

Verywellmind. n.d. "Jean's story." Verywellmind.com. Accessed 6 12, 2021. https://www.verywellmind.com/jeans-alcoholics-anonymous-story-63503.

National Institute of Alcohol Abuse and Alcoholism. n.d. "Alcohol Use in the United States." National Institute of Alcohol Abuse and Alcoholism. Accessed 6 12, 2021. https://www.niaaa.nih.gov/publications/brochures-and-fact-sheets/alcohol-facts-and-statistics.

Chapter 1

The Mayo Clinic. 2018. "Alcohol use disorder." Mayoclinic.org. https://www.mayoclinic.org/diseases-conditions/alcohol-use-disorder/symptoms-causes/syc-20369243

National Institute of Alcohol Abuse and Alcoholism. n.d. "Alcohol Use in the United States." National Institute of

Alcohol Abuse and Alcoholism. Accessed June 13, 2021. https://www.niaaa.nih.gov/publications/brochures-and-fact-sheets/alcohol-facts-and-statistics.

.Harvard science review. n.d. "The Science of Alcohol Addiction." Harvard science review. Accessed June 13, 2021. https://harvardsciencereview.com/the-science-of-alcohol-addiction/.

Watson, Stephanie. n.d. "How Alcoholism Works." science.howstuffworks.com. Accessed June 13, 2021. https://science.howstuffworks.com/life/inside-the-mind/human-brain/alcoholism4.htm.

Chapter 2

Alcohol Research Current Reviews. n.d. "Drinking Patterns and Their Definitions." Alcohol Research Current Reviews. Accessed June 14, 2021. https://arcr.niaaa.nih.gov/binge-drinking-predictors-patterns-and-consequences/drinking-patterns-and-their-definitions.

U.S Department of Health and Human Services. n.d. "2015-2020 Dietary Guidelines." health.gov. Accessed June 14, 2021. http://health.gov/dietaryguidelines/2015/guidelines.

Fort Behavioral Health. n.d. "Defense mechanisms and their role in addiction." Fort Behavioral Health. Accessed June 14, 2021. https://www.fortbehavioral.com/addiction-recovery-blog/defense-mechanisms-and-their-role-in-addiction/.

Chapter 3

National Institute of Alcohol Abuse and Alcoholism. n.d. "Alcohol's Effects on the Body." National Institute of Alcohol Abuse and Alcoholism. Accessed June 15, 2021. https://www.niaaa.nih.gov/alcohols-effects-health/alcohols-effects-body.

National Centre for Biotechnological Information. n.d. "Alcoholic Pancreatitis." National Centre for Biotechnological Information. Accessed June 15, 2021. https://www.ncbi.nlm.nih.gov/books/NBK537191/.

Drinkaware. n.d. "Alcohol and mental health." Drinkaware.co.uk. Accessed June 15, 2021. https://www.drinkaware.co.uk/facts/health-effects-of-alcohol/mental-health/alcohol-and-mental-health.

Pietrangelo, Ann. n.d. "The Effects of Alcohol on Your Body." Healthline.com. Accessed June 15, 2021. https://www.healthline.com/health/alcohol/effects-on-body.

Chapter 5

Newberg and Waldman. n.d. *Words can change your brain*. Accessed June 16, 2021.

James Clear. n.d. *Atomic Habits*. Accessed June 16, 2021.

Chapter 7

James Clear. n.d. *Atomic Habits*. Accessed June 17, 2021.

Chapter 9

WebMD. n.d. "Can Medicine Help With Alcohol Use Disorder?" WebMD. Accessed June 20, 2021. https://www.webmd.com/mental-health/addiction/features/fighting-alcoholism-with-medications#1.

Mayoclinic. n.d. "Naltrexone (Oral Route)." Mayoclinic.org. Accessed June 21, 2021. https://www.mayoclinic.org/drugs-supplements/naltrexone-oral-route/side-effects/drg-20068408.

National Center for Biotechnological Information. n.d. "Disulfiram." National Center for Biotechnological Information. Accessed June 21, 2021. https://www.ncbi.nlm.nih.gov/books/NBK548103/.

WebMD. n.d. "What Is Alcohol Withdrawal?" WebMD. Accessed June 21, 2021. https://www.webmd.com/mental-health/addiction/alcohol-withdrawal-symptoms-treatments#2.

Chapter 10

American Psychiatric Association. n.d. "What is Psychotherapy?" psychiatry.org. Accessed June 23, 2021. https://www.psychiatry.org/patients-families/psychotherapy.

Chapter 11

Very well Mind. n.d. "The Benefits of Quitting Alcohol." Verywellmind.com. Accessed June 25, 2021. https://www.verywellmind.com/what-are-the-benefits-of-alcohol-recovery-67761.

Substance Abuse and Mental Health. n.d. "2018 National Survey on Drug Use and Health." *Key Substance Use and Mental Health Indicators in the United States:*. Accessed June 26, 2021. https://www.samhsa.gov/data/sites/default/files/cbhsq-reports/NSDUHNationalFindingsReport2018/NSDUHNationalFindingsReport2018.pdf.

Printed in Great Britain
by Amazon